CHRISTMAS
with
COUNTRY LIVING
2000

CHRISTMAS
with
COUNTRY LIVING™
2000

Oxmoor
House®

HEARST COMMUNICATIONS, INC.

Christmas with Country Living™ 2000
©2000 Hearst Communications Inc., and Oxmoor House, Inc.
www.countryliving.com

Country Living™ is a trademark of Hearst Communications Inc.
Oxmoor House, Inc.
Book Division of Southern Progress Corporation
P.O. Box 2463, Birmingham, AL 35201

ISBN: 0-8487-1960-3
ISSN: 1094-2866
Printed in the United States of America
First Printing 2000

We're here for you!
We at Oxmoor House are dedicated to serving you with reliable information that expands your imagination and enriches your life. We welcome your comments and suggestions. Please write us at:

Oxmoor House, Inc.
Editor, *Christmas with Country Living*™
2100 Lakeshore Drive
Birmingham, AL 35209

To order additional publications, call 1-205-877-6560.

Country Living™
Editor-in-Chief: Nancy Mernit Soriano
Art Director: Susan M. Netzel
Managing Editor: Mary R. Roby
Deputy Editor: Lawrence A. Bilotti
Senior Editor: Marjorie E. Gage
Senior Editor/Decorating & Design: Robin Long Mayer
Senior Editor/Special Projects: Marylou Krajci
Senior Editor/Home Building & Architecture: Pamela Abrahams
Editor/Food: Cynthia N. LaGrone

Oxmoor House, Inc.
Editor-in-Chief: Nancy Fitzpatrick Wyatt
Senior Editor, Copy and Homes: Olivia Kindig Wells
Senior Foods Editor: Susan Carlisle Payne
Art Director: James Boone

***Christmas with Country Living*™ 2000**
Editor: Susan Hernandez Ray
Foods Editor: Keri Bradford Anderson
Associate Art Director: Cynthia R. Cooper
Designer: Clare T. Minges
Copy Editors: Donna Baldone, L. Amanda Owens
Editorial Assistants: Jane Lorberau, Suzanne Powell
Assistant Foods Editor: Suzanne Henson, M.S., R.D.
Illustrator: Kelly Davis
Senior Photographer: Jim Bathie
Senior Photo Stylist: Kay E. Clarke
Director, Production and Distribution: Phillip Lee
Books Production Manager: Theresa L. Beste
Production Assistant: Faye Porter Bonner

Contributors
Guest Editors: Richard Kollath, Edward McCann
Editorial Contributor: Liz Seymour
Food Stylist: Angie Neskaug Sinclair

CONTENTS

FOREWORD

Picking out the Christmas tree, planning the holiday decorations, hosting a party for friends and family—these are just a few of the pleasures of the season. Make all of your holiday preparations go smoothly with this edition of *Christmas with Country Living*.

Visit a Christmas tree farm and learn how to select and to care for a tree (pages 12–15). Next, tour the San Francisco Flower Mart, one of the country's finest open-air markets, where the best-looking decorations begin with the right materials. Then try some of our ideas for wreaths and centerpieces with naturals from your local flower mart.

For still more decorating inspiration, celebrate the season in historic North Carolina (pages 72–93). Discover some of the old-world traditions still honored in the true early American community of Old Salem. Journey with us to Seagrove, a tiny town not too far from Old Salem, where potters continue to practice a 200-year-old craft of turning red clay into beautiful handmade dishes.

Christmas just wouldn't be Christmas without the joyous custom of gathering with friends and family. Add a special touch to your parties with the luscious table settings that begin on page 100. And you'll find meal planning is simple with our mix-and-match menu on page 127.

We hope that this year's *Christmas with Country Living* makes your holiday planning easy and even more enjoyable.

THE EDITORS OF *COUNTRY LIVING*

HOLIDAY PREPARATIONS

TREES

ORNAMENTS

THE FLOWER MART

WREATHS

SIMPLE SETTINGS

CHRISTMAS TREES

IT'S THE FIRST DECISION of the holiday season: which tree to bring home. Everyone has an opinion and everyone has a say. As soon as a tree is chosen and strapped onto the car, it becomes—as every tree before it—"the best tree ever."

Before selecting a tree, make sure that you know the height of your intended room. Pick a tree that is at least a foot shorter than that height to leave space for the tree topper. Also take into account the several inches that the tree stand will add to the bottom. Trees look shorter in the open air than they do inside, so take a measuring tape with you.

Once you have picked out a tree, gently bend the branches. They should feel springy and flexible. Give the branches a shake to make sure the needles stay firmly attached. Look at the tree's color: it should be fresh, with no yellowing at the tips of the needles or the branches. Check to see that the limbs are strong enough to support ornaments. The bottom part of the trunk, or the "handle," should be straight and even. Most tree stands require six to eight inches of clear trunk; simply lop off a few lower branches to get the clearance that you need.

A fresh cut across the bottom of the trunk will help a tree absorb water and stay fresh through the holidays (above). If you are not going to bring the tree indoors immediately, cut an inch or so off the base and set the tree in a tub of water; take another thin slice off the bottom right before you bring the tree inside.

A walk through a cut-your-own tree farm on a winter's day gets the Christmas season off to a festive start. With more than twelve thousand tree farms in the United States, it shouldn't be hard to find one in your area. In addition to the wide selection of trees available, you can be certain of a farm tree's freshness. Some farms will let you tag a tree in advance and then chop it down at Christmastime. Many will cut the tree for you or at least provide a handsaw. It's a good idea to bring your own saw if you're not certain about its availability. And don't forget to bring some rope to tie the tree to your car.

The warm glow of colored lights softens the dark evergreen branches (above). Old-fashioned bubble lights (below), which were popular during the 1950s, give the appearance of candlelight.

Moravian star covers attached to twinkling lights shine brightly against the tree (above). A strand of pearl lights (below) adds interest and depth. Opposite: The flickering flames of candles attached to holders imitate the traditional method for lighting trees during the 1800s.

Trees

hristmas has its roots planted deep in ancient secular traditions that acknowledged the darkest days of winter with a celebration of renewal. Evergreen trees—proof that the cold, wintry world is not dead but just sleeping—were often an important part of such festivities. During the feast of Saturnalia, ancient Romans decorated small trees with bright bits of metal; in Scandinavia, treasures captured in battle were sometimes hung from the branches of a fir tree for good luck.

The modern Christmas tree can be traced to sixteenth-century Germany, when trees were decorated with such items as paper, apples, wafers, and sugar. The custom grew with the Paradise Tree, an evergreen tree embellished with apples used in a popular medieval play about a feast Adam and Eve held on December 24.

The spread of Christmas trees to other European nations is credited to Martin Luther, who is said to have been the first to illuminate the family Christmas tree. According to legend, he was so moved by the sight of a starry winter sky glimpsed through the trees that he wanted to reproduce the experience for his family by illuminating a tree with flickering candles. In England, however, households began decorating Christmas trees after Queen Victoria's German-born husband, Prince Albert, ordered a tree set up in Windsor Castle.

German settlers brought the Christmas tree tradition with them to the United States when they emigrated in the eighteenth century. Then in 1842, a decorated Christmas tree was introduced in Williamsburg, Virginia. The first tree lot, filled with trees from the Catskills, was established in New York in 1850.

Lighting the Christmas tree grew in popularity in the 1800s. Trees were first lit with candles that were glued on with wax or pinned to the ends of the branches. Electrical lights were used for the first time in New York in 1882 by a colleague of Thomas Edison. Colored lights were introduced in the early 1900s.

Today, the Christmas tree is a recognizable symbol of the holiday season. Personalizing the tree with traditional decorations—or family photos, as shown at right—can be a joyful celebration.

ALBUM ORNAMENTS

1 To frame your favorite photos, trim colorful textured paper with
decorative-edge scissors. If you don't want to use original photos,
make color copies. You will also need a pencil, a craft knife, a ruler,
double-faced tape, a hole punch, and string.

2 For each, place a photo on top of the mat paper. Outline the photo,
using a pencil. With the craft knife and the ruler, cut out the center
of the mat. Cut an outside border on the mat with the decorative-
edge scissors. Tape the photo to the inside of the mat and place the
mat on top of the frame paper. Using the decorative-edge scissors,
trim the frame to the desired size.

3 Tape the mat and the photo to the center of the frame. Punch a hole
at the top of the frame and the mat. Tie a length of string through
the hole to form a hanger.

THE FLOWER MART

IT'S JUST BEFORE DAWN on a chilly December morning in San Francisco's SoMa District. Elsewhere in the city, coffeepots are just beginning to perk. But here on the corner of Sixth and Brannan Streets, the business day began at 2 a.m., when the big doors opened to the 135,000-square-foot San Francisco Flower Mart. Fragrant with freshly cut flowers, potted plants, and greens from both local growers and suppliers as far away as Holland, New Zealand, and Thailand, the Mart is where florists and decorators congregate to find the city's most beautiful decorations.

Sprays of winterberries wrapped in crackling cellophane (above) brighten a vendor's stall at the San Francisco Flower Mart. Opposite: Fresh and exotic wreaths are among the items San Franciscans find to dress up their homes.

The holidays are a great time to shop the Mart—or other open-air markets throughout the country—when stalls are filled with fresh greens, blooming plants, and inventive trimmings. The San Francisco Flower Mart opens early for wholesale buyers only, but later in the day many vendors set up in the parking lot and sell directly to the public.

Wreaths at the Mart reflect the abundance of greens available in midwinter. A ring of Fraser fir (above) is decorated with pinecones and cedar. Succulents planted in soil surrounded by peat moss (below) last long after the holidays are over. Opposite: A boxwood wreath stands out against a loose arrangement of rose hips.

Hydrangeas, pepper berries, and sprays of seeded eucalyptus are set off by glossy magnolia leaves (above). A simple wreath of green bay leaves (below), an ancient symbol of honor, makes a beautiful decoration or gift. The aromatic bay leaves dry in place, creating a lovely year-round decoration.

W REATHS

WITHIN ITS NEVER-ENDING
CIRCLE, the traditional holiday wreath holds
both a welcome and a loving reminder that
Christmas rituals are part of the cycle that sustains
and warms us through the years. When you hang a
wreath on your front door, it is almost as though you
are extending an invitation to all the good spirits of
the season to come in and stay awhile.

A wreath can be loosely casual or classically
formal; made from a single variety of green berry or lavishly filled with
contrasting colors and textures; wrapped in a ribbon or left gloriously
natural. Regional materials—magnolia in the Southeast, hemlock
branches and birch twigs in New England, Douglas fir in the Pacific
Northwest—make a wreath special, but even a purchased evergreen
can be embellished with everything from bright kumquats and lady
apples to tiny ornaments.

Hang a plain Fraser fir wreath
on the door (above) or opt to
decorate it with natural materials. Opposite: A wreath of
Fraser fir and aromatic cedar is
suspended from a fir-and-cedar
garland by a string of
pinecones.

Fraser fir is an especially good choice for a wreath base because it retains its needles so well: a fir wreath will stay green from Thanksgiving until New Year's Day. Equally important, a simple fir wreath can be dressed up with other favorite and familiar greens, many of which have pleasant holiday associations. Holly, for instance, was believed by Britons to bring prosperity and good luck; ancient Romans linked ivy with feasting and drinking; and in early Europe, the pinecone, with its many seeds, was a symbol of eternity. Other common greens—juniper, with its clusters of misty blue berries, and fresh or dried magnolia leaves, with their velvety undersides showing—simply give a wonderful variety of shapes and textures to a wreath.

A wreath becomes a personal emblem of the season when it is punctuated with favorite colors and textures. Berries (above) add interest to holiday decorations. Opposite: The soft greens of chinaberry clusters and long-needled white pine set off against a background of Fraser fir contrast with the bright accents of tiny apples.

Wreaths are not just for hanging. This wreath of living succulents rooted in soil (above) circles a pillar candle.
Opposite: A sweep of heather, anchored in a ring of florist's foam, fills the top of a small tea table.

Greens are just one choice for a Christmas wreath. Dried red peppers, pale popcorn berries, dried yarrow, nuts, and seedpods make lovely and unusual wreaths. And don't forget the aromatic pleasures of natural materials: balsam, lavender, eucalyptus, and dried roses all provide a wonderful aroma in a seasonal arrangement.

From a beribboned wreath of greens on the front door to a circle of berries and dried flowers propped on a kitchen windowsill, there is no wrong place for a wreath in the holiday house. Hang a wreath in every window and over a mantel or a door; lay a wreath on the dining room table—and welcome the holidays in style.

SIMPLE SETTINGS

A LIVING PLANT at the center of a table or resting on a mantel or a windowsill brightens the short winter days. With its promise of growth and renewal and its ever-changing beauty, a blooming flower or an unfolding branch of greenery reminds us that the chilly days of winter are just a precursor to spring. Whether arranged in a group or standing alone, growing things hold a place of honor during the holidays.

The luscious flowers shown on these pages make it easy to create your own festive settings. For instance, set a bright red splash of poinsettias against a backdrop of evergreen tabletop trees. A single color display also provides great impact, such as with a bunch of red poinsettias placed in a basket. There's a special pleasure in nurturing holiday plants through the season, slowing our pace for a moment and reminding ourselves that the holidays were meant to be savored.

Bright poinsettias (above) are massed for sale. Small pots of evergreens (below) can stand alone as tabletop trees or can be incorporated into more elaborate arrangements.

Potted plants make easy and portable centerpieces that look beautiful all season. Timed to bloom during winter, paperwhites (left) lend their fragrance to the potpourri of traditional holiday aromas. Three miniature evergreen trees in a bread basket (below) look festive in an arrangement of pinecones, crab apples, and chinaberries. Opposite: A blooming orchid—a favorite year-round—takes on a Christmas air when mixed with lady apples and moss.

The contrast of white tulips against pine branches makes a soft Christmas arrangement (above). A handsome combination of poinsettias, cypress, and azaleas set off by pinecones (right) creates a nice display or an easy gift. Opposite: A pink-and-white amaryllis blooms from the top of a transferware tureen covered with Spanish moss.

COLLECTIBLES

TREASURES

STEIFF

ANIMALS

TREASURES

THE GHOSTS OF CHRISTMASES past are benign spirits indeed. Captured in antique toys and trimmings, in gently faded cards, and in carefully preserved tinsel and ribbons, they cast a warm glow over Christmas present. Whether family heirlooms or flea-market finds, vintage treasures are important touchstones that connect us to Christmases gone by.

Although trees have been dressed for Christmas since the Middle Ages, today's purely decorative ornaments are a relatively modern invention. Ornament making originated in Germany and became an important cottage-industry, supporting whole villages of artisans. With this new variety of store-bought ornaments from which to choose, Victorian families outdid themselves trimming their trees, not only with the familiar glass ornaments but also with cut- and printed-paper angels and stars, fluffy cotton Santas and snowmen, and yards of twinkling tinsel.

A winsome woman in a cotton batting dress (above) is embellished with tinsel, a holiday favorite originally invented to decorate French soldiers' uniforms. Opposite: Treasured over the years, this snowman will never melt: his body is made of cotton batting wrapped around a cardboard cylinder.

A stuffed Santa Claus and a lace-clad baby
(above) personify Christmas cheer. Such vintage figure ornaments can be quite elaborate,
often outfitted with china heads and feet.
Opposite: Fanciful glass shapes are valued by
collectors. Frequently, a family of artisans
would work together, hand-blowing glass
into molds, silvering the insides, and paint-
ing the outsides with colorful designs.

A choir of Victorian cherubs (above, opposite, and following pages) assembles to greet the holidays. So-called scrap ornaments such as these were often put together at home, using commercially produced printed designs and bits of ribbon, fabric, netting, tinsel, cellophane, and spun-glass angel hair. The ephemeral nature of these delicate ornaments makes them prized by collectors.

STEIFF ANIMALS

A PLACE OF HONOR under many family Christmas trees belongs to the gently worn teddy bear or plush elephant, passed down through the generations. The most famous playthings—and those most highly prized by collectors—are the German-made Steiff toys, distinguished by their trademark buttons in the ears. Founded in 1879 by Margarete Steiff, a seamstress who was confined to a wheelchair after contracting polio at age two, the Steiff Company has created hundreds of different kinds of animals. The earliest toys were based on drawings by Margarete's nephew Richard of real animals in the Stuttgart zoo. Cuddled and loved, played with and admired, plush animals—old and new—keep the childlike spirit of Christmas alive.

A vintage teddy bear and a more recently manufactured monkey (above and opposite) have been loved for many generations.

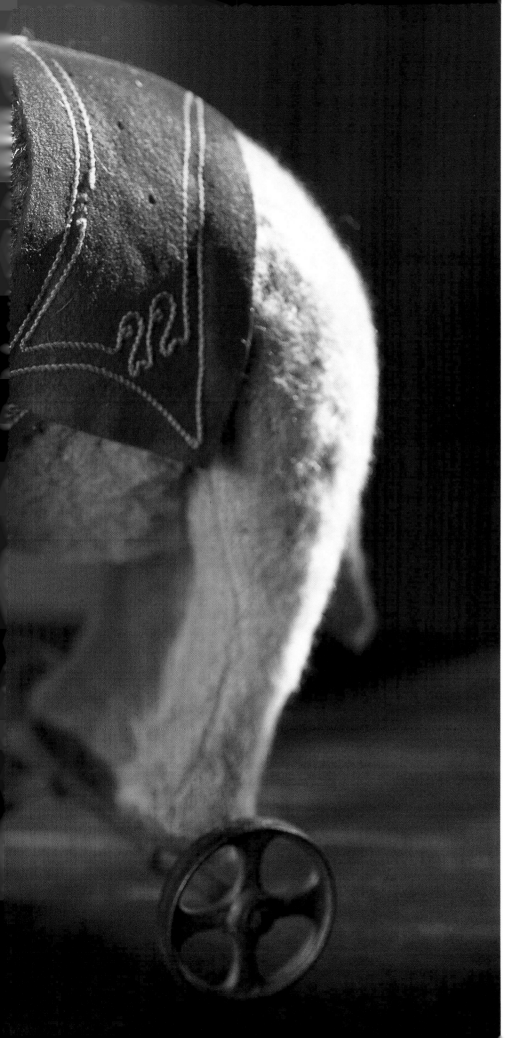

A handsome circus elephant
on metal wheels is still dressed
in its bright red blanket. Well-
preserved vintage toys such as
this command hundreds of
dollars from eager collectors.

A velvety reindeer (left) is illuminated by low winter light. Teddy bears (below) gained their name in the early twentieth century when popular president Theodore Roosevelt was photographed cuddling a bear cub. They remain the most popular type of plush toy. Opposite: A quizzical kangaroo mother and child balance on a vintage cupboard. These animals, like other Steiff creations, are made from a wide variety of tactile fabrics, including wool, velveteen, and mohair.

DECORATING

DETAILS

POMANDERS

PACKAGES

DETAILS

Tabletops, shelves, and, of course, mantels offer limitless possibilities for Christmas displays. Arrangements around the house need not be formal to be spectacular. Fruits, greenery, berries, and flowers mixed with everyday items—such as candles, vases, and bowls—create stylish holiday decorations. The combination of different textures draws out the most pleasing features of each.

Evergreens are a wonderful accent to any piece, and they'll last all season. Punctuate greens with brightly colored fruits or berries. Such fruits as apples, oranges, pears, and lemons make the best indoor decorations because they look good for several weeks without refrigeration. Fresh flowers also add color around the house. And just because it's Christmas doesn't mean you have to limit your flower choices—it's a great time to use your favorite blooms.

Above all, let the surface dictate the decoration. Hang a wreath on a cupboard door or fill a bowl with berries or fruits. Experiment with different colors and combine sizes. It's these little touches that let you know Christmas has arrived.

Candlelight illuminates lady apples, berries, and seeded eucalyptus overflowing from containers (above and opposite). The art of making fruit centerpieces can be traced to seventeenth-century France. The French crafted towers of fresh fruits "glued" together with warm caramel.

A trio of festive balls (above) are made by hot-gluing cranberries to foam. For a softer texture, tuck small pieces of moss among the cranberries. A Victorian star embellished with an angel (below) contrasts with the colorful ornaments on a small tree.

A grouping of candles towers over a tray filled with Victorian holiday crackers (above). Opposite: A tabletop tree glittering with glass ornaments crowns a sideboard's Christmas trimmings. The base of the tree rests in a woven wire urn beside handmade-paper packages (below).

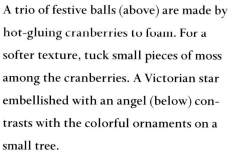

Coffee cups convert to little vases for pink
carnations (above). Opposite: The combination of flowers, limes, and holly brings the
holidays into an old-fashioned cupboard.
While flowers and citrus fruits could be used
any time of the year, the holly branches add
a bit of Christmas cheer.

Nature offers the season's finest decorations—evergreens—and you probably need not look any further than your own backyard to find them. Clipping trees and shrubs not only yields easy and inexpensive accents, but also pruning keeps the plants healthy. For even more holiday greenery, consider cutting some of the lower branches from the Christmas tree.

Each room offers unique opportunities for greenery displays. Mirrors, picture frames, and sconces are great places to tuck a few sprigs of holly or branches of pine. Such little celebrations around the house help soften winter's chill.

An antique wagon holds a quilt and a Fraser fir-and-pine wreath (below). Opposite (the types of naturals by row from top left): Fresh rosemary, anemones and Fraser fir, pine, seeded eucalyptus, holly and berries, ivy, seeded eucalyptus, variegated greens, and paperwhites all make a big impact in small places.

A pepper-berry wreath (above) hangs from a cupboard door. Pepper berries spilling from an ironstone bowl (below) complement evergreen branches and a pomegranate. Opposite: Shelves filled with greenery, berries, and fruits turn an everyday cupboard into a stunning Christmas centerpiece.

Red plums (above) bring seasonal color to a creamy bowl. A mingling of greenery and pepper berries (below) adds a splash of Christmas to the top shelf. A silver tray filled with cranberries adds a contrast of color and texture to the winter white arrangement.

Bring Christmas into the library with greenery, fruits,
and flowers. A boxwood wreath embellished with seeded eucalyptus and pinecones hangs from a ribbon
among the books (above). Opposite: Tulips in a pewter
mug sit beside an urn holding a boxwood-and-kumquat
topiary. The topiary was assembled by pressing boxwood
branches into a foam form and then securing kumquats
with florist's picks.

POMANDERS

1 To make these fragrant decorations, all you need are oranges, cloves, and a citrus stripper. (We used oranges, but this technique also works great on lemons and limes.)

2 For each, use the citrus stripper at an angle to carve designs on the orange, pulling the stripper toward you. We made a variety of swirls and crisscross patterns.

3 Complete the decoration by pressing cloves along the designs. Vary the spacing of the cloves among the oranges to create different patterns.

PACKAGES

USE GREENERY, FRUITS, AND OTHER natural materials to enhance packages. Brown kraft paper and sheer ribbon or twine make neutral backdrops for these decorative gift boxes. Scented cedar, miniature pinecones, freeze-dried oranges, and lichen produce a rustic package (top, right). A bunch of chinaberries stands out against a background of scented cedar and moss (middle, right). Pieces of manzanita centered with a pair of crab apples create a charming Christmas bundle (bottom, right). Opposite: A Fraser fir branch with a pinecone and a piece of pine accented by a golden acorn give tiny packages a simple look.

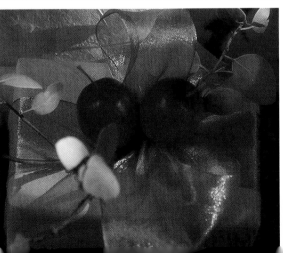

CAROLINA CHRISTMAS

OLD SALEM

SEAGROVE

REDWARE

STOCKING

OLD SALEM

Long before the clear rays of dawn touch the treetops, wood smoke rises from the chimney at Old Salem's Winkler Bakery. Across town, a musician wakes and tests the mouthpiece of his gleaming French horn. In a wintry garden, a bright cardinal plucks a berry from a sprig of holly.

It is the Saturday before Christmas in the restored Moravian village in Winston-Salem, North Carolina, and the whole community is preparing to celebrate "Old Salem Christmas." Founded by Protestant refugees who immigrated from Moravia (now part of the Czech Republic) to Germany and eventually to America, Old Salem has been refurbished as a living history museum of gardens, workshops, retail shops, homes, and community buildings.

Christmas festivities in Old Salem—the name comes from the Hebrew word for "peace"—begin in early November with a full calendar of community events and tours hosted by costumed reenactors. From early morning until dusk, visitors stroll the brick sidewalks, admiring the decorations on early nineteenth-century houses.

A Moravian star (above) is one of the simple pleasures of the Christmas season. Opposite: Sunrise illuminates Main Street, where restored shops sell Moravian goods. The brick Market-Fire House in the town commons once housed the community's horse-drawn fire engine.

In 1791, a visitor to Old Salem wrote: "The antique appearance of the houses, built in the German style, and the trees among which they are placed have a singular and pleasing effect; the whole resembles a beautiful village, and forms a pastoral scene." The Salem Tavern (right) was built in 1832 and still welcomes visitors. A handsomely restored private home (below) stands on Main Street. Opposite: A sturdy wrought iron bootscraper is bolted to a granite step (top, left). It's common to find decorative wrought iron railings on the front steps of a home (top, right). Many of Old Salem's houses are constructed of bricks made on-site from native clay (bottom, left). Just beyond a house on Church Street, the steeple of the Home Moravian Church is visible (bottom, right).

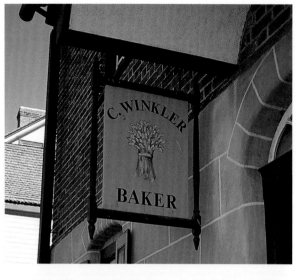

So thin they must be cut and lifted from the sheet
by hand, traditional Moravian cookies (above) are
adapted from a recipe brought to Old Salem in the
1760s. Opposite: At Winkler Bakery, built in 1807,
workers in period costumes bake sugar cakes and
bread in the original beehive oven. The Winkler
Bakery was operated by descendants of the original
Winkler family until 1927 and has been restored to
reflect Old Salem's earliest days.

Clear acrylic stars do double duty as candleholders (above) and as sparkly accents on a tree (opposite) that is also embellished with more traditional Moravian paper stars. Moravian stars are hung on the first Sunday in Advent (the fourth Sunday before Christmas) and stay up until the Festival of Epiphany on January 6. Opposite: In the simple Moravian way, the mantel in an Old Salem home is decorated with fresh greenery, pottery, and a hand-dipped beeswax candle.

The many-pointed Moravian star, some-times called the Herrnhut Star, was created in the 1850s as a geometry lesson for students at a Moravian boys' school in Niesky, Germany. One of the school's graduates produced the star commercially in the late nineteenth century; his son later founded the Herrnhut Star Factory, which supplied stars to Moravian communities around the world. Illuminated ones, like the one at the top of the tree (right), hang in windows and over doorways throughout the season. Making stars from folded strips of paper (bottom, left) is a favorite activity for children. Modern interpretations—a die-cut paper star (bottom, right) and a clear plastic star (opposite)—continue the theme.

SEAGROVE

MUDDY BOOTS LEAVE BRIGHT red footprints in Seagrove, North Carolina. The tiny town sits in the heart of Carolina red clay country, where potters have been turning that clay into jugs, crocks, and plates for over two centuries. For Seagrove's 120-plus potters, wheel-turned pottery is a generations-long tradition that began when English potters first settled the area. Other craftsmen, like David Farrell shown here at Westmoore Pottery, have come to town more recently, drawn by the community of artisans.

Bright blue North Carolina pottery decorates the top of the mantel. The mixture of large platters and small plates along with greenery and candles, adds interest and depth to the Christmas setting.

Preceding pages: The unique and varied designs of redware make it popular among collectors.

89

Redware

 eautiful redware, with its distinctive rusty color and simple decorations, was the everyday pottery of early Americans. Usually made from local clay, redware was used for everything from plates and jugs to molds, pipes, and penny banks.

Communities of any size had at least one family of potters turning out household items in red clay. Today, historians can often pinpoint the origin of a pottery piece just by its shape and decoration, since each region developed its own traditions. Pennsylvania potters made platters by draping slabs of clay over a form. Potters in North Carolina created their pieces on a potter's wheel and used a wider variety of glaze colors than their Pennsylvania counterparts.

Redware pieces from every region are decorated with delightful squiggles, perky dots, and fanciful shapes drawn in colored glaze—known as slip—applied through hollow goose quills. "The decorating has to be done fast, which makes it very free," says Mary Farrell, who operates Westmoore Pottery with her husband, David, in Seagrove, North Carolina. "It gives redware a special feeling."

For early settlers, redware had the advantage of firing at low temperatures in quickly built kilns. Clay—the same kind used to make bricks and roof tiles—was abundant in most regions. "Redware was usually the first pottery to be made when a settlement was established just because it was so easy," Mary explains. However, redware did have its disadvantages: Easily chipped, it constantly needed to be replaced. And by the mid-nineteenth century, the dangers of lead-based glazes, which react adversely with acidic foods, were well understood. At the turn of the century, yellowware and salt-glazed stoneware had taken over as the everyday china in most households.

Recently, though, collectors have rediscovered the beauty of redware's simple shapes and designs. Because it was produced in such quantities in the eighteenth and nineteenth centuries, there is quite a bit of old redware around at prices suitable for almost everyone, from less than $100 for a simple jug to over $1,000 for a highly decorated piece. At the same time, a new generation of potters, including Mary and David Farrell, are making new redware, inspired by historical models and using modern lead-free glazes.

Slip-glazed redware ornaments
brighten a Christmas tree in the dining room of a house built in 1690; the
table and the mantel display more
redware. The cheerful red on the
woodwork was inspired by the
room's original color, discovered
under 40 layers of paint. The trio of
colorful felt stockings hanging at
the fireplace recalls the appliquéd
penny rugs popular more than a
hundred years ago. Turn to the next
page for instructions on how to
make your own felt stockings.

STOCKING

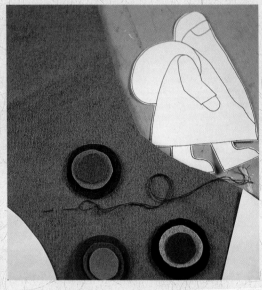

1 To make the stocking, you will need tracing paper, the patterns on pages 156 and 157, a pencil, assorted colors of felt, scissors, a needle, and assorted colors of embroidery floss.

2 Enlarge, trace, and transfer the stocking pattern to the felt. Cut two stocking pieces. Then cut a 2"x 6" rectangle for the stocking hanger. Trace and transfer the remaining patterns to the desired colors of felt; cut out.

3 Referring to the photograph on the opposite page, place the cutouts on the front stocking piece as desired. Blanket-stitch the pieces in place, referring to the diagram on page 157. Blanket-stitch the two stocking pieces together. Continue blanket-stitching along the top of the front and the back of the stocking. Fold the stocking hanger in half lengthwise and blanket-stitch along the open edge. Stitch the hanger to the inside top of the stocking.

ENTERTAINING

TABLE SETTINGS

HORS D'OEUVRES

HOLIDAY BUFFET

COOKIES

"I'll be home for Christmas," promises the old song—and of all the delights that light up the Christmas season, home glows the brightest. From Thanksgiving through New Year's Day, we open our homes to friends old and new, inviting them to share pleasures of the holiday with us. Whether we're enjoying a cup of tea for two or a dinner party for dozens, the season provides welcome occasions to renew old ties and to forge new ones.

When we can't be together, we reach out to each other by sending Christmas cards, a tradition that dates back to 1845. A peaceful wintry afternoon at the desk with a stack of cards and pretty postage stamps is sometimes almost as good as a visit with remembered loved ones.

The elegant table is set, fresh candles stand proudly in their holders, a succulent roast is in the oven, and lights twinkle on the tree. Only one task remains: the delicious ritual of deciding who will sit where and arranging place cards. Garnish table settings with place cards that are whimsical, sentimental or natural. Make your own cards with old-fashioned labels dressed up with foil seals or bright stickers (right). Then attach them to miniature bouquets, such as to paperwhites (opposite, top) or to a bundle of greenery (opposite, bottom). Or delight children—and adults—with a generous striped candy cane at each place (below).

TRANSFERWARE

CHANCES ARE THAT GRANDMOTHER'S best china was a variation on transferware. From the popular Blue Willow pattern to the exotic and often highly detailed scenes of world travel, from massive platters to diminutive doll's tea sets, transferware has been set on festive tables on both sides of the Atlantic for more than two centuries.

Transferware originated around the mid-1700s with English potters who were trying to imitate the delicate hand-painted Chinese porcelains that made their way to Europe in the holds of trading ships. The printing process used was then adopted and further popularized by Josiah Wedgwood.

Blue Willow, one of the earliest and most enduring patterns, was created in 1780 and was quickly followed by a myriad of designs illustrating such varied subjects as historical events, romantic landscapes, and scenes from popular novels.

An oval serving platter (above) is decorated with a romantic vista wreathed in flowering vines. Opposite: Transferware is printed in brown, red, purple, black, or green, as well as the traditional blue. It lends itself beautifully to mixing and matching, whether set on a table, massed on a sideboard, or displayed on a hutch.

Not as exacting as the hand-paintings that originally inspired it, transferware nonetheless required the expertise of careful artisans who could transfer engraved designs from a copper plate to a white porcelain base. Early transferware patterns were often taken directly from engraved book illustrations. After a copyright law was enacted in 1862, manufacturers began producing their own romantic designs. Nostalgic rustic scenes, such as the country farmyard shown here, were particularly popular in Victorian times, when an increasing number of people were moving to the newly industrialized cities. Brown—often called sienna—is one of the most common transferware colors, but big serving pieces in as good condition as the one pictured are relatively rare.

Preceding pages: Transferware collectors can choose from a seemingly endless selection of shapes, colors, and patterns.

In dining chairs as in table settings, a comfortable mix of well-loved antiques is often more pleasing than a matched set. A painted arrow-back Windsor chair and a birdcage Windsor chair (top, left) from the early nineteenth century beautifully complement each other. A cheerful painted country chair keeps company with a more formal Hitchcock-style chair (bottom, left), both from the mid-nineteenth century. Opposite: A sideboard is set for a buffet with an eclectic display of ironstone, creamware, transferware, and spatterware. The pieces are linked by similar colors and proportions. Tulips and greenery arranged in a tureen are an any-season favorite.

TABLE SETTINGS

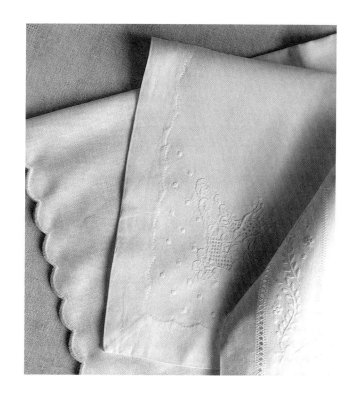

IN THE MIDST OF THE bustling holiday season, we slow down to follow the old-fashioned rituals of preparation: hand-washing the best crystal, carefully airing and ironing thick linen napkins and table-cloths, polishing the family silver to a bright shine. Like a good dinner party, an inviting table setting is worth lingering over.

Holiday entertaining is no longer an elaborate multicourse affair, but we still savor the small grace notes of the seasonal table, such as crisp linens, polished silver, sparkling glassware, and heirlooms brought out only for the most special of special occasions. There once was a time when a hostess fretted—or even trimmed her guest list—if she did not have sufficient matched place settings. In contrast, today's hostess is more likely to offer a happy mix of old and new, formal and informal, matching and almost-matching pieces—each with its own history that sparks memories and conversations.

Treated with care, table linens (above and opposite) can last for generations . Clean any stains quickly, dabbing rather than rubbing to preserve the fragile fibers. To freshen yellowed linens, wash by hand in a very mild soap-and-water solution and dry in direct sunlight.

Nothing brings the shine of the season to the holiday table quite like lovely antique silver. Mixed and matched—either by necessity or design—a variety of pieces is particularly pleasing in a special table setting. And when you get out the silver, get in some kitchen helpers. Washing, polishing, and wiping silver—with its magical ability to go from dull to gleaming—introduces children to caring for family heirlooms. Unless badly tarnished, most silver can be restored to a bright luster with an application of nonabrasive silver polish. Although more elaborately decorated pieces may need a little extra attention, most crevices can be cleaned with a dab of polish on a cotton swab or on a soft natural bristle toothbrush.

PUNCHES

WELCOME GUESTS INTO YOUR HOME this Christmas season with one of these irresistible punches. Whether you're hosting a cozy get-together or a celebration for a crowd, you'll find the perfect beverage for the occasion.

Delight coffee-lovers with decadent White Russian Dessert Punch, a smooth, rich dessert beverage made with three favorites—Kahlúa, coffee, and ice cream. It's the perfect finale to a festive dinner. Invite carolers in from the cold with warm Cranberry Cider, flavored with traditional holiday spices like cinnamon and cloves. Turn tea into a refreshing party punch—Gingered Tea Punch—by teaming it with fresh ginger and tart lemon. And find two fruity punches great for any spirited gathering: Mixed Berry-Pineapple Punch and Fruit Daiquiri.

WHITE RUSSIAN DESSERT PUNCH

(PICTURED ON FACING PAGE)

MAKES 6 SERVINGS

4 cups brewed coffee, cooled
1 quart vanilla ice cream, slightly softened
1 cup Kahlúa or other coffee liqueur
½ cup vodka
Additional vanilla or coffee ice cream (optional)

1. Combine first 4 ingredients in a punch bowl. Refrigerate at least 1 hour to allow flavors to blend. Just before serving, scoop additional ice cream into punch, if desired.

•NUTRITION INFORMATION PER SERVING—PROTEIN: 4.1G; FAT: 9.6G;
CARBOHYDRATE: 34.6G; FIBER:0.0G; SODIUM: 75MG; CHOLESTEROL: 39MG; CALORIES: 364

CRANBERRY CIDER

(PICTURED ABOVE)

CINNAMON, CLOVES, AND CRANBERRIES
GIVE THIS FESTIVE BEVERAGE ITS HOLIDAY
FLAVOR.

MAKES 6 SERVINGS

5 whole cloves
2 3-inch cinnamon sticks
2 32-ounce bottles cranberry juice
1 medium lime, cut into ¼-inch-thick slices
½ cup firmly packed light brown sugar
½ cup fresh cranberries

1. Tie cloves and cinnamon in a cheesecloth bag. In a large saucepan, combine spice bag, cranberry juice, lime, and sugar. Bring to a boil. Reduce heat to low; simmer 10 minutes. Discard spice bag. Stir in cranberries. Serve immediately.

•NUTRITION INFORMATION PER SERVING—PROTEIN: 0.1G; FAT: 0.1G;
CARBOHYDRATE: 42.5G; FIBER: 0.6G; SODIUM: 14MG; CHOLESTEROL: 0MG; CALORIES: 164

GINGERED TEA PUNCH

(PICTURED ON FACING PAGE)

MAKES 6 SERVINGS

8 cups water, divided
6 Earl Grey tea bags
1 3-inch piece gingerroot, peeled and coarsely
    chopped
1 12-ounce can frozen lemonade concentrate,
    thawed
Garnish: lemon slices

1. In a small saucepan, bring 6 cups water to a boil. Add tea bags and gingerroot. Reduce heat to low; simmer 10 minutes. Remove from heat. Remove tea bags and let tea cool to room temperature.

2. Stir in lemonade concentrate and remaining 2 cups water. Serve cold. Garnish, if desired.

•NUTRITION INFORMATION PER SERVING—PROTEIN: 0.3G; FAT: 0.2G;
CARBOHYDRATE: 28.4G; FIBER: 0.3G; SODIUM: 10MG; CHOLESTEROL: 0MG; CALORIES: 110

MIXED BERRY-PINEAPPLE PUNCH

(PICTURED AT LEFT)

IF YOU PREFER A FAMILY-FRIENDLY VERSION OF THIS FRUITY PUNCH, JUST OMIT THE VODKA.

MAKES 12 SERVINGS

2 11.5-ounce cans frozen cranberry juice cocktail, thawed
4 cups unsweetened pineapple juice
2 cups vodka
2 1-liter bottles raspberry-flavored sparkling water, chilled

1. Combine first 3 ingredients, and mix well. Refrigerate at least 1 hour. Just before serving, stir in sparkling water.

•NUTRITION INFORMATION PER SERVING—PROTEIN: 0.3G; FAT: 0.1G; CARBOHYDRATE: 15.5G; FIBER: 0.1G; SODIUM: 19MG; CHOLESTEROL: 0MG; CALORIES: 154

FRUIT DAIQUIRI

(PICTURED AT LEFT)

MAKES 8 SERVINGS

1 12-ounce can frozen orange juice concentrate, thawed
1 12-ounce can frozen pink lemonade concentrate, thawed
2 10-ounce cans frozen strawberry daiquiri mix, thawed
2 cups peach or apricot nectar
1 cup dark rum
2¼ cups water
4 12-ounce cans lemon-lime soda, chilled

1. Combine first 6 ingredients, and mix well. Refrigerate at least 1 hour.

2. Just before serving, stir in lemon-lime soda.

•NUTRITION INFORMATION PER SERVING—PROTEIN: 1.3G; FAT: 0.3G; CARBOHYDRATE: 105G; FIBER: 0.6G; SODIUM: 27MG; CHOLESTEROL: 0MG; CALORIES: 468

The secret to a perfect glass of champagne is knowing how to handle it. Place the champagne bottle on the refrigerator's top shelf for three to four hours until it reaches the ideal serving temperature of 43°F to 48°F. Serve it in wide-brimmed champagne glasses or tall, thin champagne flutes. The glasses should be very thin; thick glasses will raise the champagne's temperature.

HORS D'OEUVRES

START THE SEASON IN STYLE with an elegant appetizer party featuring champagne and caviar. Make a toast to the season; then enjoy this assortment of delicious holiday hors d'oeuvres, including Caviar-Topped Spread, Filet Mignon Crostini, and Romesco Sauce.

CAVIAR-TOPPED SPREAD

(PICTURED ON FACING PAGE)

MAKES 2 CUPS

1 8-ounce package cream cheese, softened
½ cup sour cream
¼ teaspoon salt
½ teaspoon freshly ground black pepper
3 large hard-cooked eggs, chopped
2 tablespoons chopped fresh parsley leaves
1 tablespoon chopped shallots
1 3.5-ounce jar black caviar

1. Mix cream cheese, sour cream, salt, and pepper until blended. Gently stir in egg, parsley, and shallots. Cover and refrigerate at least 1 hour.

2. Before serving, spoon into a small serving bowl and top with caviar. Serve with crackers.

•NUTRITION INFORMATION PER TABLESPOON—PROTEIN: 1.6G; FAT: 4.0G;
CARBOHYDRATE: 0.5G; FIBER: 0.0G; SODIUM: 70MG; CHOLESTEROL: 39MG; CALORIES: 44

Caviar is very perishable, and it needs to be kept well chilled even when served. For a simple, colorful presentation, choose several types of caviar—black, red, and yellow contrast nicely with each other. Place the caviar in small glass or porcelain bowls, and then place the bowls in a larger bowl filled with crushed ice. Garnish with lemon curls.

To serve, spoon the caviar on dry toast points or bland, unsalted crackers, using a nonmetal spoon. A metal spoon (even silver) will impart a metallic flavor to the delicate eggs.

QUICK BITES

When you want an easy, delicious appetizer fast, make **Bacon-Wrapped Dried Fruit.** Just cut bacon slices in half crosswise. Next, wrap the bacon around your favorite dried fruit—apricots and figs are good choices. Secure the bacon with a wooden pick, and place the wrapped fruit on a baking sheet. Broil 4 minutes; turn wrapped fruit over, and broil 4 more minutes or until the bacon is crisp.

ROMESCO SAUCE

(PICTURED ON FACING PAGE)

ROMESCO IS A CLASSIC SPANISH SAUCE TRADITIONALLY MADE WITH TOMATOES, ONIONS, PEPPERS, AND GARLIC. SERVE IT AS A DIP OR USE IT TO ADD FLAVOR TO SOUPS, PASTA DISHES, AND PIZZA.

MAKES 2¾ CUPS

1 tablespoon olive oil
2 1-ounce slices white bread
4 ounces canned roasted red peppers, drained
½ cup almonds, toasted
⅓ cup virgin olive oil
2 tablespoons red wine vinegar
1 teaspoon chopped garlic
¼ teaspoon salt
¼ teaspoon freshly ground black pepper
¼ teaspoon paprika
¼ teaspoon red pepper flakes
1 14½-ounce can diced or whole tomatoes

1. In a medium skillet, heat 1 tablespoon oil. Add bread, and brown on both sides. Tear bread into pieces; place in the jar of a blender. Add red peppers and remaining ingredients; blend until smooth. Cover and refrigerate 1 hour or overnight. Serve with crackers.

•NUTRITION INFORMATION PER TABLESPOON—PROTEIN: 0.6G; FAT: 3.0G; CARBOHYDRATE: 1.5G; FIBER: 0.4G; SODIUM: 69MG; CHOLESTEROL: 0MG; CALORIES: 34

LIMA BEAN SPREAD

(PICTURED ON FACING PAGE)

MAKES ABOUT 2 CUPS

1 10-ounce package frozen baby Lima beans,
   cooked according to package directions
⅓ cup water
⅓ cup olive oil
½ teaspoon salt
½ teaspoon freshly ground black pepper
1 clove garlic, minced

1. In the bowl of a food processor fitted with chopping blade, process all ingredients until smooth. Cover and refrigerate 1 hour or overnight. Serve with crackers.

•NUTRITION INFORMATION PER TABLESPOON—PROTEIN: 0.7G; FAT: 2.2G; CARBOHYDRATE: 2.1G; FIBER: 0.2G; SODIUM: 50MG; CHOLESTEROL: 0MG; CALORIES: 31

ROMESCO SAUCE

LIMA BEAN
SPREAD

KALAMATA OLIVE
SPREAD, PAGE 124

FILET MIGNON CROSTINI

(PICTURED ON FACING PAGE)

TENDER, JUICY FILET MIGNON TEAMS UP WITH SPICY ONION MARMALADE AND TOASTED GARLIC CROSTINI FOR A SENSATIONAL APPETIZER THAT'LL HAVE GUESTS COMING BACK FOR MORE.

MAKES 24 SERVINGS

FILET MIGNON:
2 pounds beef tenderloin
1 teaspoon salt
1 teaspoon cracked black pepper
1 teaspoon vegetable oil

TOASTED CROSTINI:
¼ cup (½ stick) unsalted butter
¼ cup vegetable oil
4 cloves garlic, minced
1 French baguette, cut into ¼-inch-thick slices
Onion Marmalade (see recipe on page 126)
Fresh thyme sprigs (optional)

1. Prepare Filet Mignon: Trim excess fat from beef. Sprinkle salt and pepper on all sides of beef. Heat a large skillet on high heat. Add oil. Place beef in skillet and sear all sides until a deep, dark surface color is reached. Reduce heat and cook, turning occasionally, 15 minutes or until a meat thermometer inserted in beef registers 145° F. Let stand.

2. Prepare Toasted Crostini: In a small saucepan, melt butter in oil and add garlic. Sauté 1 minute. Remove from heat. Cover and let stand 30 minutes. Heat oven to 350°F. Brush bread slices with garlic-butter. Place crostini on a baking sheet. Bake 10 minutes or until lightly toasted.

3. Cut beef into ¼-inch-thick slices. Place a beef slice on each crostini and top each serving with 1 tablespoon Onion Marmalade. Garnish with fresh thyme sprigs, if desired.

•NUTRITION INFORMATION PER SERVING—PROTEIN: 9.0G; FAT: 7.7G; CARBOHYDRATE: 9.4G; FIBER: 0.7G; SODIUM: 227MG; CHOLESTEROL: 29MG; CALORIES: 145

KALAMATA OLIVE SPREAD

(PICTURED ABOVE AND ON PAGE 123)

KALAMATA OLIVES—ALMOND-SHAPED OLIVES THE COLOR OF EGGPLANT—AND CAPERS DISTINGUISH THIS RICH AND TANGY GREEK-STYLE SPREAD.

MAKES ¾ CUP

1 cup kalamata olives, pitted (about 25)
2 tablespoons olive oil
2 teaspoons chopped fresh parsley
½ teaspoon capers, drained
½ teaspoon chopped fresh thyme
¼ teaspoon ground cayenne pepper
2 cloves garlic, minced

1. In the bowl of a food processor fitted with chopping blade, process all ingredients until smooth.

2. Cover spread and refrigerate 1 hour or overnight. Serve with pita wedges and crackers.

•NUTRITION INFORMATION PER TABLESPOON—PROTEIN: 0.1G; FAT: 4.4G; CARBOHYDRATE: 0.7G; FIBER: 0.0G; SODIUM: 135MG; CHOLESTEROL: 0MG; CALORIES: 42

ONION MARMALADE

(PICTURED BELOW)

MAKES 1 ½ CUPS

1 tablespoon olive oil
2 cloves garlic, finely chopped
3 medium-size red onions, thinly sliced
½ teaspoon ground cayenne pepper
1 teaspoon ground cumin
½ teaspoon salt
3 tablespoons balsamic vinegar
¼ cup firmly packed brown sugar
Filet Mignon Crostini (see recipe on page 124)

1. Heat a large skillet on medium-high heat. Add oil and garlic. Reduce heat to medium.

2. Add onions, pepper, cumin, and salt. Stir to coat onions thoroughly.

3. Stir in vinegar and sugar. Cook, stirring occasionally, until onions turn a dark golden brown and a syrupy-caramelized stage is reached—about 20 to 30 minutes. Serve with Filet Mignon Crostini.

•NUTRITION INFORMATION PER TABLESPOON—PROTEIN: 0.3G; FAT: 0.6G; CARBOHYDRATE: 4.3G; FIBER: 0.4G; SODIUM: 51MG; CHOLESTEROL: 0MG; CALORIES: 23

ORANGE-GINGER SCALLOPS

(PICTURED ABOVE)

MAKES 6 SERVINGS

ORANGE-GINGER SAUCE:
2 teaspoons finely grated orange rind
1 cup orange juice
½ cup soy sauce
2 teaspoons sugar
¼ cup chopped gingerroot

SCALLOPS:
Wooden skewers
1 pound sea scallops
¼ cup sesame oil
2 tablespoons black sesame seeds
Garnishes: orange rind curls, fresh chives

1. Heat oven broiler.

2. Prepare Orange-Ginger Sauce: In a small saucepan, bring grated rind and next 4 ingredients to a boil. Remove from heat. Cover; let steep 20 minutes. Strain, discarding solids.

3. Prepare Scallops: Soak skewers in water 30 minutes. Toss scallops in oil. Sprinkle with sesame seeds. Skewer 2 scallops onto each skewer. Place on a baking sheet. Broil 5 minutes. Serve with sauce. Garnish, if desired.

•NUTRITION INFORMATION PER SERVING—PROTEIN: 14.6G; FAT: 11.2G; CARBOHYDRATE: 11.1G; FIBER: 0.3G; SODIUM: 1228MG; CHOLESTEROL: 25MG; CALORIES: 203

HOLIDAY BUFFET

GATHER FAMILY AND FRIENDS for a holiday feast featuring these delicious dishes. You can mix and match the recipes to suit the occasion. To serve a small group of six, fix a salad, an entrée, a couple of the sides, and a dessert. When you're expecting a larger number of guests, choose all of the recipes or double your favorites to serve 12.

Several of the recipes provide make-ahead options—great for the busy holiday season. Marinate the pork tenderloin overnight; then just bake it the day of the dinner. Several hours before dinner, prepare Stuffed Chicken Breasts up to the point of baking, and refrigerate them until you're ready to bake. And keep in mind that both desserts can be prepared the day before and chilled until time to serve.

So relax and enjoy the company of loved ones over an exceptional meal meant for sharing the spirit of Christmas.

MIX-AND-MATCH MENU

SALADS
Shrimp, Grapefruit, and Avocado Salad with Honey-Tangerine Vinaigrette

Warm Salad of Apples, Walnuts, Roasted Shallots, and Cabbage

ENTRÉES
Port and Prune Marinated Pork

Stuffed Chicken Breasts

SIDES
Mixed Potato Galette

Barley Risotto

Maple-Mustard Glazed Carrots

Sautéed Brussels Sprouts with Walnuts and Red Onion

ASSORTED BREADS
French, pumpernickel, black olive, whole grain rolls

DESSERTS
Eggnog Custard Cheesecake

Christmas Trifle

SHRIMP, GRAPEFRUIT, AND AVOCADO SALAD

(PICTURED ON FACING PAGE)

MAKES 6 SERVINGS

SHRIMP:

2 quarts water

Rind from 2 tangerines

1 teaspoon salt

2 pounds raw unpeeled jumbo shrimp

SALAD:

12 ounces arugula, baby spinach, or watercress, stemmed

8 ounces frisée, stemmed

1 avocado, sliced and rubbed with lemon juice

1 red grapefruit, peeled and sectioned

Honey-Tangerine Vinaigrette

1. Prepare Shrimp: In a medium saucepan, bring 2 quarts water, tangerine rind, and salt to a boil. Add shrimp and cook 3 to 4 minutes or until shrimp turn pink. Drain; peel and devein shrimp. Chill.

2. Assemble Salad: Arrange arugula, frisée, avocado, grapefruit, and shrimp on a platter. Serve with vinaigrette.

•NUTRITION INFORMATION PER SERVING—PROTEIN: 25.4G; FAT: 29.5G; CARBOHYDRATE: 12.1G; FIBER: 0.8G; SODIUM: 785MG; CHOLESTEROL: 172MG; CALORIES: 411

HONEY-TANGERINE VINAIGRETTE

(PICTURED ABOVE AND ON FACING PAGE)

MAKES ABOUT 1 1/4 CUPS

1/4 cup fresh tangerine juice (1 large tangerine)

1 tablespoon honey

1/4 cup white wine vinegar

3/4 cup peanut oil

1 teaspoon salt

1/2 teaspoon freshly ground black pepper

1. Process first 3 ingredients in a food processor until blended. With blender on, slowly add oil; process until well blended. Add salt and pepper and blend.

•NUTRITION INFORMATION PER TABLESPOON—PROTEIN: 0.0G; FAT: 8.1G; CARBOHYDRATE: 1.2G; FIBER: 0.0G; SODIUM: 118MG; CHOLESTEROL: 0MG; CALORIES: 77

Warm Salad of Apples, Walnuts, Roasted Shallots, and Cabbage

(PICTURED BELOW)

MAKES 6 SERVINGS

¼ cup apple cider vinegar

½ teaspoon salt

¼ teaspoon ground black pepper

¼ teaspoon chopped fresh thyme

⅓ cup canola or vegetable oil

4 shallots, peeled and quartered lengthwise

3 Granny Smith apples, cut into eighths and cored

3 cups julienne-sliced savoy cabbage

1 cup julienne-sliced red cabbage

½ cup coarsely chopped walnuts

½ cup grated Asiago cheese

1. Heat oven to 400°F. In a jar with a tight-fitting lid, combine cider vinegar, salt, pepper, thyme, and all but 1 tablespoon of the oil. Shake well and set aside.

2. Toss shallots in a large mixing bowl with the reserved 1 tablespoon oil. Place shallots on a 10- by 15-inch jellyroll pan and roast 12 to 15 minutes.

3. Add apple slices to shallots and roast 15 minutes more. Toss cabbages and walnuts together and add to shallots and apples.

4. Pour dressing over all of mixture in jellyroll pan and toss well. Roast 7 minutes more. Sprinkle with Asiago cheese. Serve warm.

•NUTRITION INFORMATION PER SERVING—PROTEIN: 6.4G; FAT: 20.0G; CARBOHYDRATE: 17.6G; FIBER: 3.2G; SODIUM: 321MG; CHOLESTEROL: 5MG; CALORIES: 261

PORT AND PRUNE MARINATED PORK

(PICTURED AT RIGHT)

MAKES 8 TO 10 SERVINGS

MARINADE:

2 cloves garlic, minced

1 tablespoon grated orange rind

2 cups ruby port

¾ cup chopped prunes (4 ounces)

2 tablespoons chopped fresh rosemary leaves

12 whole black peppercorns

1 teaspoon salt

PORK:

1 3- to 3½-pound boneless pork loin roast

1 14.5-ounce can beef broth

½ cup fresh cranberries

1 tablespoon cornstarch

¼ cup fresh orange juice

Garnishes: orange wedges, fresh rosemary,
    fresh cranberries

1. Prepare Marinade: In a medium saucepan, bring all marinade ingredients to a boil over medium heat. Reduce heat to low and simmer until prunes soften—about 5 to 7 minutes. Let cool to room temperature.

2. Prepare Pork: Place pork in a 2-gallon heavy-duty plastic food storage bag; carefully pour in marinade. Seal; refrigerate overnight, turning bag occasionally.

3. Heat oven to 375°F. Remove pork from plastic bag and reserve marinade. Place pork on a wire rack in a roasting pan. Insert a meat thermometer into thickest portion of pork. Roast pork until thermometer registers 160°—about 1 hour. Let stand 10 to 15 minutes before slicing.

4. Pour reserved marinade and beef broth into a medium saucepan (add any drippings from pork roast). Bring to a boil over high heat and add cranberries. Reduce heat to medium and cook, stirring often, until cranberries pop. Strain and return to saucepan. Combine cornstarch and orange juice; add to saucepan. Bring to a boil. Boil 1 minute to thicken, stirring constantly. Remove from heat. Serve on the side with pork roast. Garnish, if desired.

•NUTRITION INFORMATION PER SERVING—PROTEIN: 41.6G; FAT: 7.0G;
CARBOHYDRATE: 13.7G; FIBER: 0.7G; SODIUM: 443MG; CHOLESTEROL: 125MG; CALORIES: 289

Step 1   Step 2   Step 3

STUFFED CHICKEN BREASTS
(PICTURED ON FACING PAGE)

MAKES 6 SERVINGS

6 large boneless, skinless chicken breasts halves
    (about 2 pounds)

½ teaspoon salt

½ teaspoon freshly ground black pepper

2 cups thinly sliced white button mushroom
    caps (6 ounces)

2 medium-size red pears, peeled and shredded

4 ounces goat cheese

1 teaspoon finely grated lemon rind

1 large egg

1 tablespoon water

1⅓ cups packaged unseasoned bread crumbs

½ cup grated Parmesan cheese

All-purpose flour for dusting

Olive oil-flavored cooking spray

1. Place chicken on a sheet of plastic wrap; cover with another sheet of plastic wrap. Pound to ¼-inch thickness, using the flat side of a meat mallet or a rolling pin (**see Step 1 photo**). Remove top sheet of plastic wrap; sprinkle chicken with salt and pepper and set aside. Place mushrooms and pears in a medium skillet and cook over medium heat 8 to 10 minutes, stirring occasionally. Remove from heat and let cool to room temperature.

2. Combine the mushroom-pear mixture, goat cheese, and lemon rind. Divide filling evenly among chicken breasts and spread evenly over a third of the surface of each breast. Fold chicken breasts in half to cover filling. Secure with a wooden pick (**see Step 2 photo**).

3. In a small bowl, combine egg and 1 tablespoon water. In a shallow bowl, combine bread crumbs and Parmesan cheese. Dust each folded breast lightly with flour and dip into egg mixture, moistening all surfaces. Coat with bread crumb mixture, patting crumbs gently in place (**see Step 3 photo**). Place chicken on a large baking pan. (The chicken can be prepared to this point several hours ahead; cover and refrigerate. When ready to cook, let chicken stand at room temperature 20 minutes.)

4. Heat oven to 375° F. Spray each chicken breast with cooking spray. Bake 25 minutes or until done, turning chicken halfway through cooking.

•NUTRITION INFORMATION PER SERVING—PROTEIN: 45.6G; FAT: 10.6G;
CARBOHYDRATE: 31.1G; FIBER: 2.4G; SODIUM: 847MG; CHOLESTEROL: 147MG; CALORIES: 409

MIXED POTATO GALETTE

(PICTURED ABOVE)

MAKES 6 TO 8 SERVINGS

¼ cup (½ stick) unsalted butter
¼ cup vegetable oil
3 bay leaves
4 cloves garlic, minced
2 pounds (6 medium) Yukon Gold potatoes
2 pounds (2 to 3 large) sweet potatoes
Salt
Freshly ground black pepper
Garnish: fresh bay leaves

1. In a small saucepan, melt butter with oil. Add 3 bay leaves and garlic. Bring to a boil. Remove from heat. Cover and let stand 30 minutes to infuse butter. Meanwhile, peel and thinly slice potatoes (see Step 1 photo). Discard bay leaves from butter.

2. Heat oven to 350°F. Line bottom of a 10-inch cast-iron skillet with parchment paper (see Step 2 photo); brush paper with infused butter.

3. Layer Yukon Gold potatoes in a concentric circle, overlapping each slice slightly (see Step 3 photo). Brush with infused butter and sprinkle lightly with salt and pepper.

4. Layer sweet potato in same fashion; brush with butter and sprinkle lightly with salt and pepper. Continue layering process, alternating Yukon Gold and sweet potato layers (see Step 4 photo). Drizzle remaining infused butter over top layer and press down on top to compress layers. Sprinkle lightly with salt and pepper.

5. Bake, uncovered, 1 hour or until top layer is crisp. Remove galette from skillet by carefully flipping it out onto a serving dish. Garnish, if desired. Serve warm.

•NUTRITION INFORMATION PER SERVING—PROTEIN: 3.7G; FAT: 12.9G;
CARBOHYDRATE: 30.9G; FIBER: 4.0G; SODIUM: 38MG; CHOLESTEROL: 16MG; CALORIES: 248

Step 1: After peeling potatoes, thinly slice them, using a mandolin (shown above) or a sharp knife. A mandolin is a handy machine for cutting firm vegetables such as potatoes into uniform slices. You can find mandolins at specialty kitchen shops and large department stores.

Step 2: Draw a 10-inch circle on a piece of parchment paper, using your cast-iron skillet as a guide. Cut out circle and place it in the bottom of the skillet.

Step 3: After brushing the parchment paper with the infused butter, layer the Yukon Gold potato slices in a circle; continue layering until the bottom of skillet is covered.

Step 4: After brushing the first potato layer with the infused butter and sprinkling it with salt and pepper, repeat the layering procedure with the sweet potato slices. Repeat both potato layers.

BARLEY RISOTTO

(PICTURED BELOW AND ON PAGE 132)

MAKES 6 SERVINGS

4 cups chicken broth

3 tablespoons vegetable oil

1 cup chopped fennel

1 cup medium onion, finely chopped

1 cup uncooked pearl barley

2 cups peeled, cubed butternut squash (1-inch cubes)

½ teaspoon salt

¼ teaspoon freshly ground black pepper

1 teaspoon chopped fresh sage

2 tablespoons chopped fresh parsley

2 tablespoons half-and-half

⅓ cup pine nuts, toasted

Garnish: fennel leaves

1. In a medium saucepan, heat broth.

2. In a large nonstick skillet, heat vegetable oil. Stir in chopped fennel and onion and cook until softened—about 5 minutes. Stir in barley and squash. Sauté 2 minutes to coat lightly with oil. Sprinkle with salt and pepper.

3. Ladle hot broth into barley mixture, 1 cup at a time. After each addition, stir well and allow barley and vegetables to absorb the broth. Continue stirring and adding broth until barley is tender—about 20 minutes. Stir in sage, parsley, and half-and-half. Sprinkle with toasted pine nuts. Garnish, if desired. Serve immediately.

•NUTRITION INFORMATION PER SERVING—PROTEIN: 9.5G; FAT: 16.4G; CARBOHYDRATE: 39.6G; FIBER: 7.3G; SODIUM: 732MG; CHOLESTEROL: 2MG; CALORIES: 323

Maple-Mustard Glazed Carrots

(PICTURED ABOVE AND ON PAGE 132)

MAKES 6 SERVINGS

1 pound small, thin carrots with tops
1 tablespoon butter
1 tablespoon Dijon mustard
¼ cup maple syrup
2 tablespoons orange juice
¼ teaspoon salt
¼ teaspoon pepper
Butter (optional)

1. Trim carrot tops, leaving ½ inch of green tops attached. Cook carrots in boiling salted water 5 to 8 minutes or until crisp-tender; drain and set aside.

2. Melt 1 tablespoon butter in a large nonstick skillet over medium-low heat. Add mustard, maple syrup, and orange juice and cook, stirring constantly, until butter melts and ingredients are well combined.

3. Add carrots, stirring until well coated. Reduce heat to low and cook until carrots are tender—about 10 minutes. Sprinkle with salt and pepper. Top with a pat of butter, if desired. Serve immediately.

•NUTRITION INFORMATION PER SERVING—PROTEIN: 0.9G; FAT: 2.3G;
CARBOHYDRATE: 16.4G; FIBER: 1.1G; SODIUM: 237MG; CHOLESTEROL: 5MG; CALORIES: 86

Sautéed Brussels Sprouts with Walnuts and Red Onion

(PICTURED ON FACING PAGE)

SAUTÉEING ENHANCES THE FLAVOR AND COLOR OF BRUSSELS SPROUTS WHILE RETAINING THEIR NUTRIENTS. A GLASS TRIFLE BOWL IS AN IDEAL WAY TO SHOW OFF THIS BRIGHT VEGETABLE.

MAKES 6 SERVINGS

2 pints Brussels sprouts

2 tablespoons butter

½ teaspoon salt

½ teaspoon freshly ground black pepper

2 tablespoons chopped walnuts

2 tablespoons minced red onion

Grated lemon rind from ½ lemon

1 tablespoon lemon juice

1. Trim bases off Brussels sprouts. Cut sprouts in half and place, flat side down, on a cutting board. Cut into fine shreds, starting at base.

2. Heat butter in a 10-inch skillet over medium heat. Add Brussels sprouts, salt, black pepper, chopped walnuts, and red onion.

3. Sauté mixture until Brussels sprouts are crisp-tender. Remove from heat and stir in grated lemon rind and lemon juice. Serve immediately.

•NUTRITION INFORMATION PER SERVING—PROTEIN: 1.6G; FAT: 5.4G; CARBOHYDRATE: 3.4G; FIBER: 1.4G; SODIUM: 241MG; CHOLESTEROL: 10MG; CALORIES: 64

Bountiful Breads

Offer an assortment of breads as part of your holiday meal. Choose a variety of loaves such as whole grain, pumpernickel, French, black olive, and sesame loaves for rustic appeal. And, best of all, you don't need to spend a lot of time in the kitchen. Just stroll through your supermarket's bakery section or make a trip to your favorite bakeshop. Dress up the breads by displaying them on a colorful cake stand or on a Christmas platter.

Eggnog Custard Cheesecake

(PICTURED ABOVE AND ON FACING PAGE)

MAKES 8 SERVINGS

VANILLA WAFER CRUST:

1 cup crushed regular or reduced-fat vanilla wafers
   (25 wafers)

¼ teaspoon ground nutmeg

¼ cup (½ stick) unsalted butter, softened

FILLING:

2 8-ounce packages Neufchâtel cheese (⅓-less-fat
   cream cheese), softened

¼ cup sugar

1 tablespoon cornstarch

3 large eggs

3 tablespoons light rum or ¼ teaspoon rum extract

⅛ teaspoon salt

1¼ cups low-fat sour cream

1½ cups refrigerated eggnog

⅛ teaspoon ground nutmeg

Sweetened whipped cream (optional)

Freshly grated nutmeg (optional)

1. Prepare Vanilla Wafer Crust: Heat oven to 325°F. Process wafer crumbs, nutmeg, and butter in a food processor until well blended. Press onto the bottom of a greased 8-inch springform pan or cake pan with removable bottom. Bake 10 minutes and cool on wire rack.

2. Prepare Filling: In a heavy-duty electric mixer with paddle attachment, beat cream cheese until soft and pliable—about 3 minutes. Add sugar and beat another minute. Beat in cornstarch and eggs, one at a time, beating only until eggs are incorporated. Stir in rum, salt, and sour cream until thoroughly blended. Stir in eggnog and nutmeg. Pour batter into prepared springform pan.

3. Bake at 325° for 1 hour and 5 minutes or until almost set (center will still jiggle slightly but will firm up upon cooling). Turn off oven, open oven door slightly, and let cheesecake stand in oven 30 minutes. Remove cheesecake from oven. Let cool to room temperature on a wire rack. Cover and refrigerate until cold—several hours or overnight. When ready to serve, run a knife around edge of cake. Remove sides of springform pan and place cheesecake on a serving platter. Garnish with whipped cream and nutmeg, if desired.

•NUTRITION INFORMATION PER SERVING—PROTEIN: 11.5G; FAT: 31.6G;
CARBOHYDRATE: 24.6G; FIBER: 0.4G; SODIUM: 380MG; CHOLESTEROL: 182MG; CALORIES: 439

CHRISTMAS TRIFLE

(PICTURED AT RIGHT)

MAKES 16 SERVINGS

CUSTARD:

5 cups milk

1 cup sugar

½ cup cornstarch

½ teaspoon salt

4 large egg yolks

2 teaspoons vanilla extract

TRIFLE:

¼ cup seedless raspberry jam

2 12-ounce pound cakes, cut into ½-inch-thick slices

¼ cup curaçao or brandy

4 oranges, peeled and sectioned

4 kiwifruit, peeled and diced

1 pint raspberries

1 cup heavy cream

1 tablespoon confectioners' sugar

¼ teaspoon vanilla extract

Garnishes: raspberries, fresh mint sprigs

1. Prepare Custard the day before assembling and serving: In a 4-quart saucepan, combine milk, sugar, cornstarch and salt. Bring to a boil over medium heat; boil, stirring constantly, until thickened. In a small mixing bowl, whisk egg yolks; whisk in 2 cups milk mixture. Whisk egg yolk mixture into remaining milk mixture in saucepan; cook 3 minutes more. Remove from heat and stir in 2 teaspoons vanilla. Immediately cover surface of custard with plastic wrap, and refrigerate overnight.

2. Prepare Trifle the next day: In the bottom of a 4-quart glass trifle bowl, spread a small amount of the jam. Arrange about 4 slices pound cake on the jam, cutting as necessary to completely cover the bottom of the bowl (**see Step 1 photo**). Brush cake with curaçao or brandy (**see Step 2 photo**). Brush with jam. Arrange a third of the orange sections, half of the kiwifruit, and half of the raspberries over the jam (**see Step 3 photo**). Arrange a third of the orange sections against the glass bowl in a decorative pattern. Spread half of the chilled custard over the fruit. Top with the remaining pound cake slices. Brush with curaçao or brandy, then jam. Top with the remaining orange sections, kiwifruit, raspberries, and custard. Cover trifle with plastic wrap and refrigerate several hours.

3. Just before serving, whip cream with confectioners' sugar and ¼ teaspoon vanilla. Pipe over trifle in a decorative pattern (**see Step 4 photo**). Garnish, if desired.

•NUTRITION INFORMATION PER SERVING—PROTEIN: 4.9G; FAT: 14.5G; CARBOHYDRATE: 37.8G; FIBER: 2.1G; SODIUM: 192MG; CHOLESTEROL: 124MG; CALORIES: 306

Step 1: Spread jam in the bottom of a 4-quart trifle bowl. Layer about 4 pound cake slices over the jam. (You may need to break a slice into pieces to fill in the spaces between the cake slices.)

Step 2: Brush the pound cake layer with curaçao or brandy, using a pastry brush.

Step 3: Layer the orange sections, kiwifruit slices, and raspberries over the pound cake layer. Arrange some orange sections around the bowl in a decorative pattern. Top all the fruit with half of the custard. Repeat the layers.

Step 4: Pipe sweetened whipped cream over the trifle in a decorative pattern, using a pastry bag. Garnish with fresh raspberries and mint sprigs, if desired.

COOKIES

SHARE THE WARMTH OF THE HOLIDAYS with a personal gift of home-made cookies. These recipes make it easy. Just start with the basic dough for Butter Cookies, and modify the ingredients a little as directed in the other recipes. The results? Fabulous cookies that are sure to become new holiday favorites.

Butter Cookies are always a welcome classic, but when you want something different, try Kringles. Caraway seeds, almonds, and brandy help create a delicious treat that adults will love. And children will be delighted with Fruit-Filled Turnovers. The apricot and raspberry fillings and sprinkling of confectioner's sugar make these cookies irresistible.

Impressive-looking Checkerboard Cookies are really a snap to make, especially when you follow the simple step-by-step photos. And there's even an all-chocolate variation (pictured above) for chocolate fanatics.

Best of all, you can make these cookie doughs ahead and freeze them. Then you'll be able to bake made-from-scratch cookies in a matter of minutes for a Christmas party or a spur-of-the-moment present.

BUTTER COOKIES

(PICTURED ABOVE)

MAKES 48 COOKIES

3 cups unsifted all-purpose flour
1 teaspoon baking powder
½ teaspoon salt
1 cup (2 sticks) unsalted butter, softened
1 cup sugar
2 large eggs
2 teaspoons vanilla extract

1. Sift together flour, baking powder, and salt; sift again. Set aside. In a heavy-duty electric mixer with the paddle attachment, beat butter on medium speed until light and fluffy—about 3 minutes. Add sugar and beat 2 minutes more. Beat in eggs and vanilla. Reduce speed to low; gradually beat in flour mixture until dough forms. Wrap in plastic wrap and refrigerate at least 1 hour or overnight. (Dough may be frozen for 3 weeks; then thaw in the refrigerator.) Use cookie dough to make the 3 cookie variations that follow this recipe. Or, to bake plain butter cookies, continue with step 2.

2. Heat oven to 350°F. Roll out the dough to ¼-inch thickness on a lightly floured work surface or between 2 pieces of waxed paper. (If dough gets too warm and sticky, rewrap in plastic and refrigerate until it is firm enough to roll.) With a 2½-inch round cutter, cut dough into 48 circles. Place 1 inch apart on ungreased cookie sheets.

3. Bake cookies until edges of cookies begin to brown—10 to 12 minutes. Let cool slightly on cookie sheets; then transfer to wire racks to cool completely.

•NUTRITION INFORMATION PER COOKIE—PROTEIN: 1.1G; FAT: 4.1G; CARBOHYDRATE: 10.2G; FIBER: 0.2G; SODIUM: 38MG; CHOLESTEROL: 20MG; CALORIES: 82

KRINGLES

(PICTURED AT RIGHT)

MAKES 48 COOKIES

1 recipe Butter Cookies dough
¼ cup brandy
½ cup finely chopped blanched almonds
2 tablespoons caraway seeds

1. Prepare dough as directed, increasing flour to 3¾ cups, baking powder to 1 tablespoon, and sugar to 1¾ cups. Add brandy alternately with flour mixture. Knead almonds and caraway seeds into dough after all flour mixture is added. Shape dough into two 3- by 6-inch logs. Wrap logs in plastic wrap and freeze until firm—at least 2 hours.

2. Heat oven to 375°F. Cut each log crosswise into twenty-four ¼-inch-thick slices; place on ungreased cookie sheets. Bake until edges are lightly browned—about 10 to 15 minutes. Let cool slightly on cookie sheets; transfer to wire racks to cool completely.

•NUTRITION INFORMATION PER COOKIE—PROTEIN: 1.6G; FAT: 4.9G;
CARBOHYDRATE: 15.3G; FIBER: 0.5G; SODIUM: 59MG; CHOLESTEROL: 20MG; CALORIES: 111

FRUIT-FILLED TURNOVERS

(PICTURED AT RIGHT)

MAKES 72 TURNOVERS

1 recipe Butter Cookies dough
⅓ cup seedless raspberry jam
⅓ cup apricot jam
¼ cup confectioners' sugar

1. Heat oven to 350°F. Divide dough in half. Wrap one half in plastic wrap and refrigerate. Roll other half of dough to ⅛-inch thickness. With a 2½-inch round cutter, cut out twenty-four circles. Place a scant ½ teaspoon raspberry jam onto center of each circle and fold in half, pressing edges together. Repeat with remaining half of dough, using apricot jam.

2. Place turnovers on ungreased cookie sheets. Bake until edges are lightly browned—about 13 to 15 minutes. Let cool slightly on cookie sheets; transfer to wire racks to cool completely. Sprinkle cooled turnovers with confectioners' sugar.

•NUTRITION INFORMATION PER TURNOVER—PROTEIN: 0.7G; FAT: 2.8G;
CARBOHYDRATE: 8.2G; FIBER: 0.3G; SODIUM: 27MG; CHOLESTEROL: 13MG; CALORIES: 61

CHECKERBOARD COOKIES

(PICTURED ABOVE)

MAKES 48 COOKIES

1 recipe Butter Cookies dough (see recipe on page 146)
2 ounces unsweetened chocolate

1. Divide cookie dough in half. Wrap one half in plastic wrap and set aside. Place chocolate in the top of a double boiler and let melt over simmering water, making sure the water does not touch the bottom of the bowl containing the chocolate. Let cool. Knead the chocolate into half of dough, forming a chocolate dough (**see Step 1 photo**). Shape the chocolate dough into a 1- by 2- by 12-inch rectangle. Cut in half lengthwise to form two 1- by 1- by 12-inch rectangles. Repeat shaping procedure with the vanilla dough. Place 1 length of chocolate dough beside 1 length of vanilla dough and press together lightly (**see Step 2 photo**). Place the remaining length of chocolate dough on top of the first length of vanilla dough. Place the remaining length of vanilla dough on top of the first length of chocolate dough (**see Step 3 photo**). Press all lengths together lightly. Wrap in plastic and chill until firm—about 1 hour.

2. Heat oven to 350°F. Unwrap dough and cut crosswise into ¼-inch-thick slices (**see Step 4 photo**). Place on ungreased cookie sheets. Bake until edges of cookies are just lightly browned—about 10 to 12 minutes. Let cool 1 to 2 minutes on cookie sheets; then transfer to wire racks to cool completely.

•NUTRITION INFORMATION PER COOKIE—PROTEIN: 1.2G; FAT: 4.7G; CARBOHYDRATE: 10.6G; FIBER: 0.2G; SODIUM: 38MG; CHOLESTEROL: 20MG; CALORIES: 88

Variation: To make an all-chocolate version, use 4 ounces chocolate. Knead as directed in Step 1, but use all of dough. Wrap dough in plastic wrap; refrigerate at least 1 hour or overnight. Roll out dough to ¼-inch thickness on a lightly floured work surface. With a 2½-inch round cutter, cut into 48 circles. Place 1 inch apart on ungreased cookie sheets. Bake until edges begin to brown—10 to 12 minutes. Cool slightly on cookie sheets; transfer to wire racks to cool completely.

Step 1: Knead the melted chocolate into half of the dough, forming a chocolate dough.

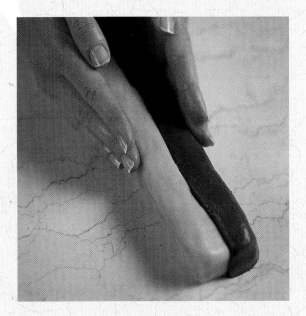

Step 2: Place 1 length of chocolate dough beside 1 length of vanilla dough and press together lightly.

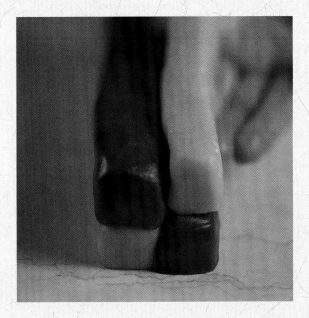

Step 3: After placing the remaining length of chocolate dough on top of the first length of vanilla dough, place the remaining length of vanilla dough on top of the first length of chocolate dough. Wrap in plastic wrap, and chill

Step 4: Unwrap chilled dough and cut crosswise into ¼-inch-thick slices. Place on ungreased cookie sheets and bake as directed.

Introduce an unusual custom at a holiday gathering this year: a Peppermint Pig™. The Peppermint Pig comes with a little bag and hammer (opposite). You place the pig inside the bag and let guests take turns cracking it with the hammer (top, right). Once the pig is shattered, everyone can sample a piece of the pig in hopes of good luck in the following year (bottom, right). The Peppermint Pig is also accompanied with a sheet explaining the legend of the pig (see Resources on page 156).

Peppermint

AN ESSAY

othing sums up the sights, the tastes, and the smells of Christmas quite like the slender candy cane. Fragrant with peppermint, bright with crisp stripes, and bent into a graceful curlicue, the candy cane is a cheerful symbol of the sensory delights of the season.

The modern candy cane dates from 1670, when the choirmaster of Cologne Cathedral in Germany crooked the ends of a batch of sugar candy sticks in the shape of a shepherd's staff and distributed the sweet treats to children during the nativity service. The charming custom caught on and spread rapidly throughout Europe. In northern Europe, the canes were sometimes further embellished with sugar roses at holiday time.

German settlers brought the candy cane tradition to America, adorning their holiday trees with the then-all-white canes. The first historical record of a candy cane in the United States—dated 1847—describes a tree in Wooster, Ohio, decorated by German-Swedish immigrant August Imard, who hung candy canes and handmade paper ornaments on a blue spruce.

No one knows exactly when the candy cane gained its stripes, but it was probably around 1900. Christmas cards before that date show only white canes, but cards printed afterward depict the familiar striped cane. Around that same time, peppermint and wintergreen—familiar in Victorian households as herbal remedies and flavors for tea—were added to the Christmas candy cane. They remain the classic flavor combination.

Until the 1950s, candy canes were pulled, twisted, cut, and bent by hand in family kitchens or at local confectioners' shops. With the development of an automated candy cane machine and special boxes for packing and shipping the brittle candies, candy canes became a familiar symbol of Christmas in every region of the country.

Today, candy canes are sold in a dizzying variety of colors, flavors, and sizes. The old-fashioned striped peppermint cane remains a perennial favorite, though, whether tucked into the bow of a holiday package, hung from the end of an evergreen bough, or found peeking out of the top of a child's stocking on Christmas morning.

RESOURCES

Artisans

Birdhouse Brokerage
(rustic birdhouse, pages 2–3)
P.O. Box 466
Poughkeepsie, NY 12602
(877) 895-1496
birdhous@frontiernet.net
www.birdhousebrokerage.com

Candles

Illuminations
1995 South McDowell Boulevard,
    Building A
Petaluma, CA 94954
1-800-CANDLES
www.Illuminations.com

Primavera, Inc.
312 Michigan Avenue
Decatur, GA 30030
(404) 373-3914
Fax: (404) 373-3914

Candy

Michael's—The Candy Corner
(handmade candy canes, pages 101,
    153)
www.candycornerusa.com

Saratoga Sweets
(Peppermint Pig™, pages 150–151)
1733 Route 9
Clifton Park, NY 12065
1-800-827-9060
www.peppermintpig.com

Decorative Papers and Wrapping Supplies

Cardrageous
345 West Manhattan
Santa Fe, NM 87501
(505) 986-5887
Fax: (505) 988-2358
www.cardrageous.com

Caspari
35 East 21st
New York, NY 10010
(212) 995-5710

Dick Blick Company
P.O. Box 1267
Galesburg, IL 61401
(309) 343-6181

Kate's Paperie
561 Broadway
New York, NY 10012
1-888-941-9169
Fax: (212) 941-9560
Send $3.00 for catalog.

Loose Ends
P.O. Box 20310
Keizer, OR 97307
(503) 390-7457
www.4loosends.com
Send $5.00 for catalog.

Fabric and Thread

The DMC Corporation
(embroidery floss #498, #729, and
    #935, pages 94–95)
South Hackensack Avenue, Bldg. 10A
South Kearny, NJ 07032
(973) 589-0606
www.dmc-usa.com

National Nonwovens
(wool felt, pages 94–95)
180 Pleasant Street
Easthampton, MA 01027
1-800-333-3469
www.nationalnonwovens.com

Fresh Evergreens

Bald Mountain Farm
P.O. Box 138
Todd, NC 28684
1-800-577-9622 or 1-888-611-2129

Battenfeld & Sons Christmas Trees
(Christmas trees, pages 12, 14, 15)
P.O. Box 856, Route 199
Red Hook, NY 12571
(845) 758-8018

Laurel Springs Christmas Tree Farm
P.O. Box 85
Highway 18 South
Laurel Springs, NC 28644-0085
1-800-851-2345

Fresh Plants and Wreaths

Bloom-Rite Brand® by Nurseryman's Exchange
(tiny evergreen trees and flower
    plants, pages 33, 34, 35, 37)

Paul Ecke Ranch
(poinsettias, pages 33, 37)
P.O. Box 230488
Encinitas, CA 92023
1-800-468-3253
www.ecke.com

Silver Terrace Nurseries
(flowers and wreaths, pages 22–25)
652 Brannan Street
San Francisco, CA 94107
(415) 543-4443

Lights

Kurt Adler/Santa's World
(lights, pages 16, 17)
www.kurtadler.com

Linens

John Matouk & Company
(monogram napkin, page 110;
    napkins, pages 111, 117;
    place mats, pages 150–151)
37 West 26th Street
New York, NY 10010
(212) 683-9242
www.matouk.com

White on White
(hand towel and coasters, page
    110; tablecloth, page 144)
888 Lexington Avenue
New York, NY 10021
(212) 288-0909

Old Salem Decorative Arts and Baked Goods

Old Salem, Inc.
(dishware and cookies, page 79;
    stars, lights, plates, lanterns, table,
    chair, and basket, page 80; stars,
    pages 82, 83)
P.O. Box F, Salem Station
Winston-Salem, NC 27108
1-888-653-7253
www.oldsalem.org

Ornaments

Smith & Hawken
(glass balls, pages 19, 20)
1-800-940-1170
www.smithandhawken.com

Thumbprint Antiques
(antique ornaments, pages 40, 43)
P.O. Box 159
Stone Ridge, NY 12484
(845) 687-9318

Pottery

Potluck Studios
(flowerpot, page 62; punch bowl,
    page 114; linens and dishware,
    page 116; compote, page 120;
    platters, pages 128, 130; cake
    stand and candlesticks, page 139;
    plate, page 140; cake stand, page
    141; linens, pages 146, 147, 148)
23 Main Street
Accord, NY 12404
(914) 626-2300

Westmoore Pottery
(pottery, pages 84, 86–87, 91)
4622 Busbee Road
Seagrove, NC 27341
(910) 464-3700

Ribbon

Offray Ribbon Company
360 Route 24
Chester, NJ 07930
(908) 879-4700
Fax: (908) 879-8588
www.offray.com

ACKNOWLEDGMENTS

COUNTRY LIVING WOULD LIKE TO THANK THE MANY HOMEOWNERS,
DESIGNERS, AND ARCHITECTS WHOSE WORK APPEARS ON THESE PAGES.

Photography
Keith Scott Morton, pages 62 (lower right),
    88–89, 92–93
Courtesy of Old Salem, page 74

Homeowners and Contributors
Arlene and Gregory Chiaramonte

William Cissna
Al Gonzalez
Ann Johnson
Celia and Marshall McGarity
Jane and Steve Schneider
Louise Strutner

PATTERNS

STOCKING INSTRUCTIONS ARE ON PAGE 94.

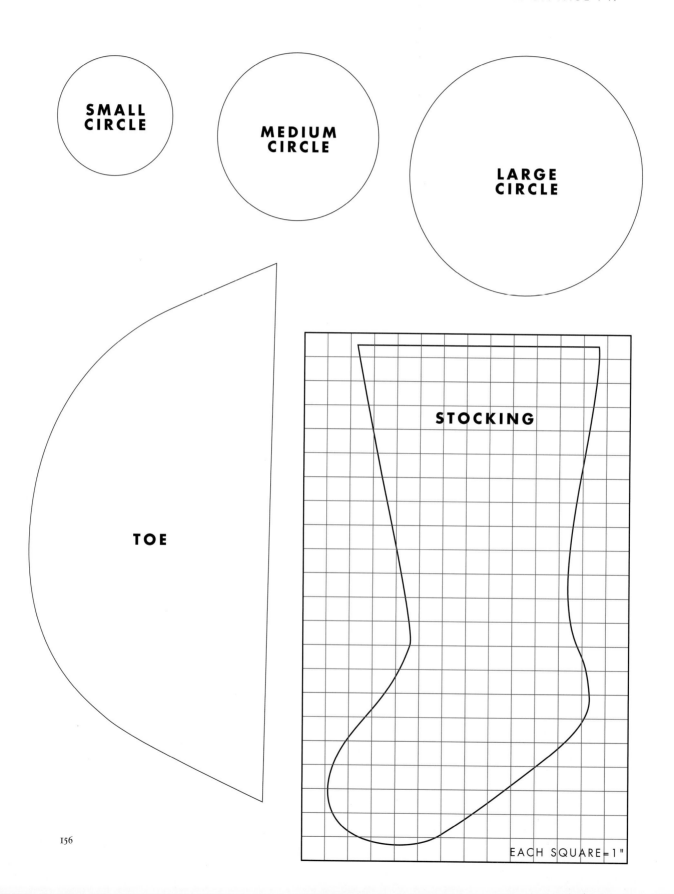

SMALL CIRCLE

MEDIUM CIRCLE

LARGE CIRCLE

TOE

STOCKING

EACH SQUARE=1"

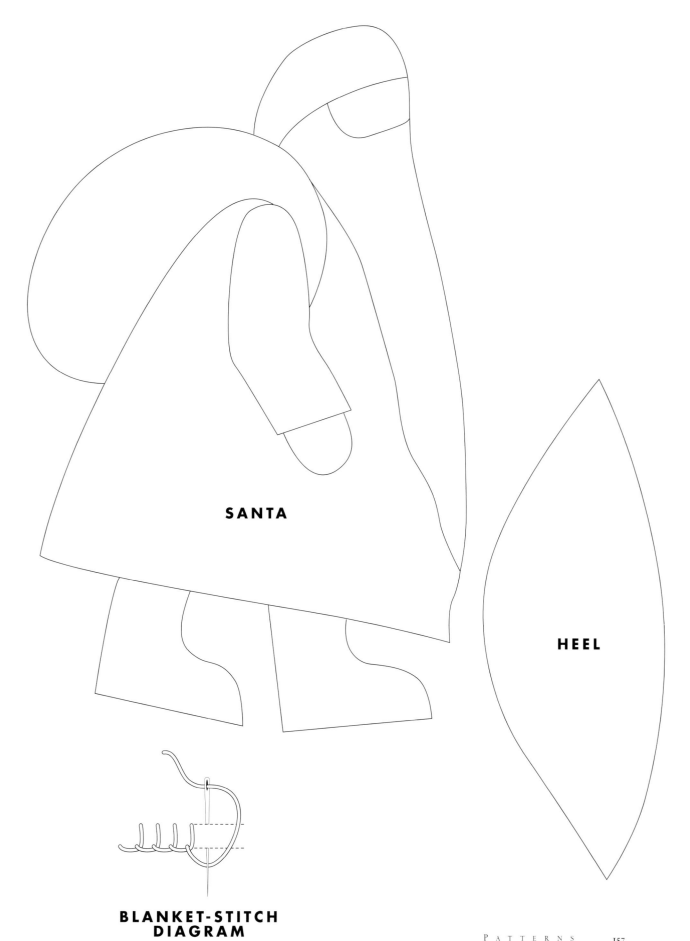

SANTA

HEEL

BLANKET-STITCH
DIAGRAM

INDEX